fovos

johnny legnard

fovos

johnny legnard

contents

short story

our fathers

i watch cloud faces in the sky
yelling, shouting in terror

what a *horrific* thing to see looking down on me

fall

look through, deep past her eyes
a spider lives in here

dying

youth is fleeting
what the hell am i to do
if it wasn't for time, i could be as young as i want
though, still i age onward
onward towards old age and death
i know all this
but
what
the hell
am i
to do

age

they say that time is an illusion
but look at what it does to us

gift

thank you for making me an artist
it's such a beauteous story

the mall

sitting in your car tonight
living out this moment in life
loving every inch upon your face
you could be my goodnight
and i would be your sunrise
you could be my complexity
and i would be your sad poetry
you could be happy
and i could be happy
or one of us could just be sad

little winter

i'm only leaking through the telephone

i fell in love with every word i said

you sound like one of those falsetto girls

the muffled air blowing in my ear

i have never been in love before *you*

you're a hot soul and a hot contender

could you still deny our little winter

what a shame, for we were just brilliant

faking it

let's act like
people in public
get along
and speak of nothing
buckle down
until we master it
then go home
and hibernate together
it's without doubt
my favorite tune
and you, my dear
are the lyrics i've memorized
i hold my breath
amongst all others
but with you
i can truly breathe

ugly mouth

i watch her, the un-fairest of them all but not completely
despicable
with lips of a frown, a pallet so wide, her ugly past
completes her complexion
not but a second thought will hold her to me, or another
for that matter
she slams them down
awaits the effects
celebrity will always be within her
i watch her as she claims to watch me or another for that
matter
her brain is not of stature but tis not light in terms of
consistency
so my words hesitate to pass my teeth when around her
but still, she slams them down
no consequence seems to await her
from the glass to her hideous mouth she slurps and
swooshes around 13%
the frown is in full effect, drowning her chin into her
neck
empty lips separate gasping for attention
i watch her, disgusted, appalled, and horrified
i turn to a liquid fire jacket
the sleeves are warm, my chest ignites, and my face is
fast asleep
the room is cast upon swells and to catch my feet, hands
are to no use
i stumble true, land amongst a dame in which i fall
ugly mouth of horrid hall, redesigned as a fair maiden
her lips are perked, her chin is sharp, and her eyes are
cat-eyes
she walks about with an aura of invincibility and
mandatory consideration
nay, requirement

oh, i watch her now, she parades about, listing in
perfection, causing a scene
mingling with undesirables and non-worthies then
staggering off to keep up appearances
i polish my glass to drink into beauty but i come up dry
i turn again to cast eyes on the reborn Venus
how now could i shut them after such progress
shall i run for the hills or wait it out
though, i fear in great distress what awaits my hangover
a hideous, wretched, monstrous appearance of a woman

remaining quiet

i really aim to practice humility

and feel i do all right

but now, half way there

i have nothing to show anyway

whether that be the case

or i'm just too sick to know

please don't forget about me when i'm gone

delusional thoughts

as of late, it has found me in my adrenaline adventures
but i sit in the donut and i scream through the page
anyway

*what if she had sweet berry-skin and i had the last crave
in the world*

heathens

this is as far as we go
no one can question us why
living as demons and drowning like seaman
no one to inherit the sky

kill

i wish i could eat all your pain and ride 180 miles per
hour, crashing into a brick wall

nympho

her eyes are like two shallow pools of blue
they make you want to dive in head first

she will slay you with the look in her eye
and she lives down town

her word is all in all, all i need
deep pits of tentacles and paler francais

she will slay you with the look in her eye
and there is danger down town

her and her royal God-complex
it's even worse when she brings in her mother

she will slay you with the look in her eye
and i'm going down town

she still wants it
(she says)
lay me down, and i will save you
(i say)
baby, you get me high

life of love

we are put on this earth to fall in love and break hearts
to crave happiness and be depressed

then tragically *die*

wasted time

every day i want to confess my love for you
       even though it may be imprudent
you know this, you're the greatest player
       how many months or years has it been now
how much more dead are we

    but romance is such a beautiful game

mother bird

do you know why the mother bird sings in the night
she frets for her baby in leave for a flight
a beautiful song is sung and is heard by all creatures
sleeping astone
alone
tis a darker night in a deeper fright
and nothing but sadness is sung to Lazarus
oh, nothing tonight
no hope in sight
oh mother bird, singing a tune in hopes to cradle baby
soon
be all right, be all right mother bird, oh, be all right
it's okay to hurt and to cry
but still, you'll sing alone into the bite of the night
you'll sing alone under the cold, damp sky
until your voice can hold no tune anymore
until your eyes and neck and stomach sore
your love and care and anger quake
your heart and soul and spirit break
when fear and grief and sorrow win
the loss of love will then set in
and now silent is the night as nothing is bright
no, not tonight mother bird, not tonight
oh, i'm sorry mother bird
but not tonight

your man

let him take your breath away
as he doesn't listen and brushes off his shoulder

the mask

come out with me tonight so that one day i can ignore
you while gazing out the window

all women

i know you're in love with him
he treats you like *shit*

power trip

her lips feel so kind to my kiss
and her tongue is a taste of sweet, wet softness
i can't wait to land upon her neck and breath in her
racing heart
it's all so magical and makes me religious
i can feel her *verve* pulsing through my veins and i feel
unstoppable
she is the source to my power

paradise

i didn't hear what you said to me
did you even say anything

at all

beauty queen, you're a scene
don't you think that they had enough

you're crime, girl

you talk 'till you suffocate
we connect but we don't relate

your eyes give you away

i love visitors all the time
but they can never stay too long

say "*hi*" to your friend

xxx

i don't know her name
but i love her face
she's always mine
in computer space

and that chronic glare
lost inside her eyes
i wish I was there
deep within her thighs

give it to me, babe
until you've had enough
call me by my name
and then i'll fall in love

alone in my room
listen to you speak
looking really smooth
as you *come* to me

cold touch

let it out little honey
give it up on a sunday
breathe it all in and just let it go

take it up if you're able
lay it out on the table
some day you will find peace in all this

even though you're my baby
it's okay if you hate me
i'm not feeling so hot but girl, I know that ain't all you
got

at the top of your lungs
scream in its face
if i gave you a gun
would it help to erase

when it's dead

i can hardly wait

through the door, the breeze calls me

time slows and then stops

dogs

i'm more of a lone coyote, not so impressive but, sad
       and desperate to find connection
from hunter to scavenger, i fall from rank
       as prey turns into scraps and leftovers
my new diet allows me to fast
       and it doesn't bother me as i'm gluten-free
a few good years of friends and the hunt until we stray
       a week later, i die

fate of the monster

you're into *loving*
maybe you'll love me

hunt me to town
hunt me down

i'm in the know a lot
you beg to differ

come gather 'round
watch a man *drown*

a while longer

i've been all around the world
and still i'm not on your mind
i've been waiting here for some time
and i'll be here for a while longer

memory is fast asleep
and signs are becoming clear
all desires are shrouded in fear
and there are faces in the water

romance has gone away
somewhere i can't reach
over mountains and seas
though, the music will go on

a long journey plays
but i will see no rest
until i'm at my best
and your days will turn to nights

old man was right again
still i just don't seem to hear
all my closest friends are right near
but i'm leaving in the morning

i can still see her face
i'm haunted by every cry
make it last and hold it close and tight
though, i'll never see the day

listening to you breathe
is like it's sung from an angel
and my eyes on your eyes and a kiss
sounds like heaven to me

taketh away from you
and lay it all on me
i pray, that's why i live
and your nights will disappear

wait a moment

we have the basis for a perfect romance
but i'd throw it all away to fall in love
if i close my eyes i can believe it's true
though, in reality, i've learned raw poetry

i feel so close yet so far away
and now i finally understand that
a spider in danger is a spider that bites
though, in safety, she is still so dangerous

i'm dying, i'm fading, *i am suffocating*
so dreaming of a break of tears, i will surely drown
without my sidearm i'm nothing but anxious
complete me and i'll complete you, i swear

waiting

i'm on to something, though, alas i succumb to malady
of weakness and dire urgency through claws of grief

distress will come to all in forms of melancholy
not shallow of time nor aura of kin will bring relief

in some kind of daze, a love encased in sugar-flesh
disaster eyes have sung sweet dreams of harmony

all that is young in beauty set designed to leave us
with not but a fright ever feared, save for worry
will be the death of me

cowboy death

upon your luck, amid your lies
i've long desired to put a hole between your eyes

i'm into it, but you're afraid
this is your final chance to turn and walk away

most come to play to slay the game
i'm warning you, i've come to do the same

and now here we are, ready to play
call unto you as i am here to stay

ghost story

the only ghost whom i'll ever fear
holds my gaze from behind the mirror
hooked on nearly every shade of blue
heart to heart, really is love true

i feel left out in the morning time
it conjures up then becomes a rhyme
i hear the steps walking on the floor
they tip-toe by heading out the door

the only ghost whom i'll ever know
is the only one who will ever show
give me passion, give me loving
give me pain just give me something

the only ghost who has more to pay
is the lonely one who has left to say
"you're the apple of my eye"
you're the joke that just won't die

we sit around in the la-de-da
then go on about the bla bla bla
it doesn't really matter how it's said
in the end we're all as good as bread

the pleasure hides well deep within
it rises out and sleeps in the skin
glances pass through gaze-less eyes
mock in love is screams and cries

i bought a dollar with just one hat
it's nothing great, it's exactly that
it's cheap

the only ghost whom i'll ever love
is the only one i'm capable of
read it through back from the start
if you can't discern it just call it art

last art

i see the world on fire, but all the time
i see the earth in tears, drowning
i see my mom and my dad
and my sisters and friends, in the worst
and my hands have arthritis
and my hands are in pain
i'm sick and tired of writing and painting
i'm sick and tired of line to rhyme
i can write through the cramps
i can soak the page
but it doesn't put the fire out

jab baby

while yesterdays have all but been forgotten
and you just can't remember how to love me

we can still talk on the phone 'cause i'm not worried
i'll just play as your friend and rob my own time

banana chapstick left a taste in my mouth
as if you don't know what i'm up to, girl

i'm much better now, deep into my acting
because you're only *sad* if you have tears

strange days and long nights out of breath
i'm much better now that i have poetry

and sting does my ear when i hear and say your name
i'd write it down if i could ever manage it

can you remember the night of a thousand lights
oh, my whispering girl

i'm a student, i'm an actor, i'm an artist
i am much better now

but of course it rains today

schoenfeld

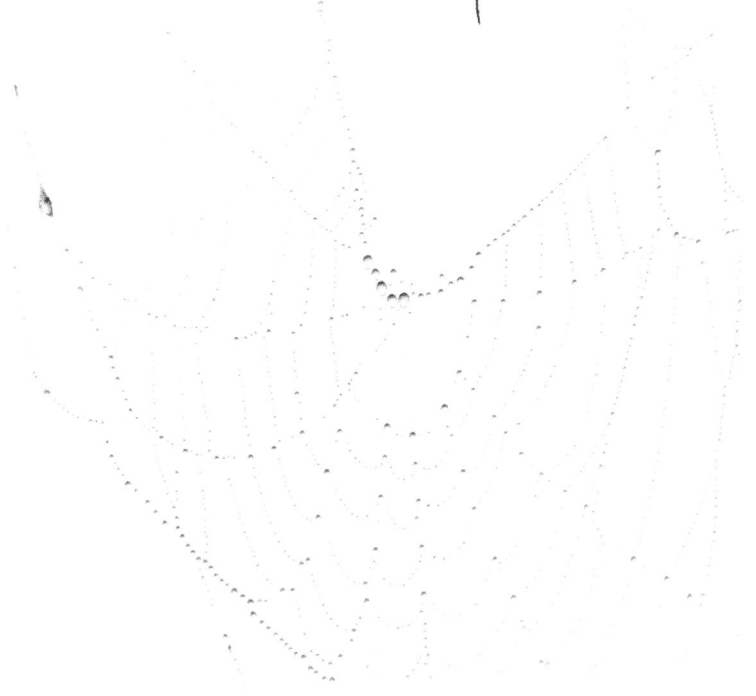

Photo 1

"The Smoker"

It's been a long deep breath since *Nightwatchers,* a breath I've longed to keep. There's nothing I can say bad about it, though, I do feel this artistic tribulation nonetheless. I pace about the premier in conflicted thought, perplexed by these immense feelings of doubt. My mind is a scatter-box mixed with negative, anxious tension ready to burst and then implode, leaving me as a crack in existence. I'm around but I'm hardly present as I swig a 40% distilled elixir, pursuing a calm of nerves and peace of mind. Talk chatters on my ear but I hear nothing. It's loud and obnoxious with little sense about it. The sea of consumers gathers around and form committees. They dare not venture out and mingle into the fray. It's much safer and easier to converse with the bodies you arrive with. Though, as it is, it seems the crowd is in high spirits, as unto me, I retreat back into my classic despair.

The *time* before our new film was a fear-ride that kept me feeling out of sorts. I was lost, more than usual, I confirm, and only a blast of cure-ray would be my savior. The months leading up to my creative conundrum was only a way through black night and ultimate confusion. This dread set in as an indefinite host and began clawing away at the controls. I've been completely re-wired. I can hardly think, let alone eat or breathe. Desire was my opposite-friend terrorizing the Townsend and replacing him with a Being more competent and appealing. "It's been a long day" I would try to convince myself, though, day indeed, it hasn't been long in time. What has become me? Interest fades and I'm reminded of the lackluster deed of performing. Does this really mean nothing? What does it mean to me? Does it matter what I think? The impending doom collapses lower, threatening now with an Adams-apple of concentrated saliva, in fear of a break to clear its throat, I would surely escape. Though, I wouldn't. In complete panic, I rush over to my effects and begin a run-away pile. I don't know where it is I'm going, or for how long, but I need to leave now! It's a bright and dreary day, as of old, it's a tradition I've "longed" to keep. I pack my car as high as a couple bags, leaning in to fit the musical valuables (I seem to be less hideous with these notes of pure therapy). I'm off, speeding as fast as I can move. What next? The question barely enters my mind. It's a rid of a "long day" and I'm happy it's close to expiring. I sink back into the home where I belong. It's better here, and somewhat safer, though I can't put my finger on it. Time passes as I tend to my wounds, I'm an actor, I can "act" like I'm unaffected. As I role play, I begin to think, what is it I must occupy my time with? This takes a toll on me, all the while, my old friend Creativity comes in with a suggestion. "Build, make, create!" he says. My response is no longer immediate. I fear to wind up in old fashion, only to drop way low, capsize and drown.

Whether I heed consciously to these creative endeavors, I complete the action nonetheless, filling my fragile mind with stories and projects. Completely on their own, they come up with a beginning, middle, and end, expecting me to lead them into battle. I'm unsure what to do though. I've been attending tribulation, remember? So, I begin to sift aimlessly. I meander. I head into the mountains searching for peace, not as a narcissist, but as a young man, learning to breathe again. As I try and accept my new life, the brilliance of the world must intervene. An old friend writes me, this time a real person, suggesting we get together and catch up. We'll call him Dylan, mainly because that's his name. With a new, soothed mind, I respond and accept to his proposal.

This is where he and I started working on our latest project. I suggested this wacky idea, Dylan very much enjoyed it, we made magic happen. All the while, the feelings of tribulation persisted. I assured them they will be addressed though, not during this odyssey. Like a young, misbehaved child, these feelings continued to pester me. Little do they care, as I be a man of trouble, alas, consistency has been the name of the game, and despair, the essence. Though, question me not, I remain and toil. As a new group ventures into the unknown, we come out as a unit, victorious. The real magic has taken effect. We live and die in this night at the premier. The heart is sewn on a screen, then enters the eyes of the unready. A new beginning and a new belief is set alight inside these unknowing passengers. They also live and die on this night, and as the last committee joins and embraces, we unite as one.

Though, when times of joyous endeavors and little smiles are over, I remain here. In this place of uncertainty. Here in this place of un-want. Here alone. I retire back to my post. The walk from my car to the house is pleasant but short lived. I trail about the abode. I scour for food. I eat. Time rolls by as I'm left to the mercy of my mind. Mindless television remains black and broken. My trusty phone glued to my hand finds its place back to where it belongs. Hovering over my lap. I fire it up and begin my curious search. All site platforms are mine and in the palms of my hands. Though I've been lucky to remain reluctant to such mind controlling, brain washing sites such as "Instagram" still, I respond to its beck and call. I have no immediate business about this foreign land, no responsibility. My interest in others lacks creativity. It's cold inside and black and pretentious. I care not for the traditional, daily escapades that is food-photography or self-loved, self-modeling. Something must be here for me to become. A thought strikes my mind. What are the kings of old, high school champions dominating now?

I search through nostalgia, looking up names to find familiar faces. It's a laugh! There's nothing familiar about these fat faced, sin indulging, gluttonous, anti-heroes of the past. I hardly recognize the captain of the water polo team without his scepter in hand, though, only to be replaced by an affordable way to become inebriated. My mind is a merry-go-round. I'm not even sure what to feel. I delve deeper and deeper into the memory of past happenings. What I ultimately find is something that disturbs me on a whole new, soul sinking level. SCHOENFELD. Katie Schoenfeld. I remember her as one of the popular girls in 7th grade in whom banished me to the hounds of lesser. As a young boy, hearing the words "Like him, he's ugly" hardly blends well with a face to face confrontation and a point of the finger. Not that I let something so minute as my "placement" in middle school take heed on the rest of my experience. It's not like I became weirdo or succumbed further to introversion. I wasn't that all black wearing, long haired, music blasting theater kid. I had yellow shoe laces.

Schoenfeld. Something about her profile pic created a downhearted response in my soul. A selfie. A selfie of Katie smoking a cigarette. Not that smoking is the oddity standout point to this dilemma. It's the way her eyes seem sunk and the bags that carry with. It's the gaze-less disconnect that pierces through. Her skin of white, pale, unhealthy, dry. Lips in the way I seek to please, pleads no man. Dread is about her. Do I dare dive into this pit? Shall I continue on? Yes. I click on her profile and up pops the rest of her ghastly, unsightly digital celluloids. I'm horrified. I don't remember her this way at all! Who is this girl? She is not the same person I remember, casting me off as she once has. There's something darker to her now. In all her photos, death is her stare. Bland is her aura. An invisible grip grasps her spirit but I can't put my finger on it. Depression? Illness, possibly mental? Drugs? That's got to be it. Drugs. I read through her captions. They're not as adoptable as others may be. I continue my read as I find the factor in which disturbs my core. Repeated comments by others (assuming they're friends of her's) on a photo posted back in December of 2016, her last post. "Hey Katie, we miss you". "Where ever you are, we hope you're safe". Then a young man who's seemingly remained consistent in her comments (I know from my quick research on her account) writes "Hey Katie, I miss you. I'm out in the Bay area right now but plan to move south by the 14th or 15th. I'm doing better now. I love you, where ever you are, I hope you're happy."

I'm not completely sure as to why but, fear and dread has overwhelmed myself. What has happened to her? Is she hurt? Is she sick? Is she alive? Who is this man? A lover? A fighter or tyrant? I feel scared for this girl. It's not a fear I can admit to being relatable. It feels less like fear and more like depression. I'm sure my current, unstable state hasn't helped ready me for this dark, new update. Why do I take this personal? Why can't I shake it? It's the same wicked feeling as that of a horrible nightmare. I'm trapped. I'm deep in a hole. This overwhelming notion of rescue takes over my body. I should just turn off my device and call it a night. But how now? I'm living through anxiety; how should I now expect nothing less than a black pursue of night? I'm unhappy. More than before. I'm unwilling. More than before. The only thing on to me now is to find this girl. I must find this girl. I must rescue Schoenfeld.

Photo 2

"Starbucks Bathroom Selfie"

A sleepless night of tossing and turning and dreaming through despair and horror and the like. The clock says 4. 4:00 am, I presume as it's still dark out. No outcome of return to Z's in which I will avail. "Here comes the day" says the chill of the morning. An abhorred day to those aware of Schoenfeld. Without a second thought or break of feast, I saddle up my day's uniform. Marching around my quarters, I begin to conjure a plan. An idea that is wound tight in my loose, scattered mind (these are how ideas normally come to me. I usually have no say in the matter. I must let it run its course.) But much unlike an idea, this thought seems to be pressing on me. On my soul. It's urgent and relentless. It's confusing and tiresome. I search for my side arm and send out a call to Dylan. We agree to set a meeting to go over this new, intruding idea of mine. Though, before I leave, I must sneak another peek at Schoenfeld's account.

Bleak. So bleak. Again I'm stricken with the same deep purple. I march through her photos, this time trying to achieve a higher understanding of her style. I come across a starchy post, her taking a mirror selfie in what appears to be a public restroom. It's nothing unbecoming. But oddly enough, her phone intentionally covers her face. Her outfit isn't anything special, and I wouldn't go as far as saying she had an amazing due (though I'm a guy, and this could all be subjective). It's almost psychopathic in a strange sense. The restroom is dim lit, as the available neon rays struggle to reach the other side of the already small, single toilet room. It's blue. It's a dark and faded blue. The mirror is slightly dirty but not a mess. The walls are of Grey tones. She hardly stands out from the wall behind her. I take it all in. Really trying to understand this. Perhaps I'm delving too deep into what is probably just another stupid selfie, you may say. But I don't care what you think.

As difficult as it is to move my eyes from the damn photo, I turn to scroll down to view the caption. "I am brave to use Starbucks' bathroom, and free Wi-Fi is a plus." What the hell does that even mean! This is a perfect example of "delving too deep" but the ambiguity of this perplexing, vague caption boggles my damn mind! "I am brave" Why? Why is she brave? Starbucks? What is so bloody terrifying about Starbucks' restrooms? Is there something I don't know? What the hell! I can't figure this thing out. Is it the fear/ phobia of using a public facility? Is she afraid that someone will hear her, see her? And what about the second part of that stupid caption. "and free Wi-Fi is a plus." What does that even have to do with the first damn part of her mindless utterance? "free Wi-Fi is a plus"? A plus for what? What the hell does any of this mean? My mind falls to the floor. I try to make sense of this senseless act. Does none of her facilities work in her home? Does she go to Starbucks for hygienic and internet purposes? Is she homeless? She doesn't look homeless. She looks bleak but not homeless. Mentally exhausted and nearly spent, I've previously made arrangements with Dylan that I must follow through with. I pack my things along with my baggage and head out.

It's been a good 20 something minutes since my "freak out" and now I'm beginning to feel "not as bad". The short drive to the yet achieved destination is enough to slightly calm my nerves. Instead of just Dylan, I'm meeting with most of the crew. Though the anxiety has subsided, in no way has it been subdued. But I'm an actor, I can "act" like I'm unaffected. When I show up, most everyone is already there. Obviously Dylan. Isaac (My close friend and fellow actor/ artist.) Chris (An old friend and cinematographer of *Nightwatchers* and various other projects.) Cassie (An artist of diverse talents, one being painting, Dylan's girlfriend/ a new friend.) And Corbin (A sketch artist and Dylan's younger brother, he can be my friend too.) I take a deep, relaxing breath and make my way to the group... Action.   I spend what feels like hours talking about this new insanity. In short. I propose that we make a mockumentary (mock documentary) of the possible deep happenings of Schoenfeld's account life. In the mockumentary, I would take a "film crew" with me as I try and track her down. In the end we would find if she was dead or alive. Hopefully the latter. Dylan has suggested that we throw in a twist but, we haven't yet thought of anything. The film would be about me coming up with this idea, writing it, then we would improv all the scenes, though, we'd have them solidly structured. After some time of this anxious subject, Dylan and the rest of the crew move the topic to another current film in which we are all working. But not me. I sit quietly. It's manic but only inside. As they're lips continue on, they forget they're words. It's silent and slow motion. I'm segregated from the committee. I just can't remove myself from the possible truth of the actuality of Schoenfeld. This once horrible teenager "Like him, he's ugly" is now possibly swept away by an evil I just can't seem to even begin to try comprehending. I have no ill feelings of that what has been said in the past. I care not.

I return to my phone. Again with her profile. It's deep and immense, riddled with tragedy. My heart turns upside-down. I do my best to hide my true feelings. Photo after photo after photo after photo after photo. Bleak. So bleak. In my new scavenge, I return to the consistent commentator. The one who wrote "I love you... I miss you... I'm doing better now... bla bla bla." We'll call him @papadiam, mainly because that's what he calls himself on this God forsaken site. @papadiam is everywhere in her content. He's a mess too. Every other comment is "I love you" or "I miss you" or "I'm doing better". All joking aside, this fiend is scary. I navigate to his profile and commence a new research. Fear strikes my heart as it would in the hearts of all men. I scour through his photos, collecting every bit of information possible. A killer. Or something of one in the making. His body is shredded like that of an athlete. Tattoos on his self is a must, and unintelligent ones at that. His choice of wardrobe is ill informed and that of a mistake, sporting wrestling t's and baggy jeans, all choked off with a gold necklace. Marijuana and possible other drugs on display. I pull down further into his resume and find what could be considered as a mentally inept, hillbilly functioning arsenal. Multiple photos of assault rifles and all different pieces. As for the quality of his photography, one could make the connection that he's indeed in possession of all these weapons rendered by his glass skills and choice of backdrop.

As I read further, something disturbing in an opposing manner presents itself. His mother has recently passed away (from what I gather). Utterly unfortunate as I take this to heart and I feel for this monster for a moment. I continue reading. Almost in every single post (photo) he mentions his dead mother. But not in a way of felt sorrow, but in pure passion. He presents himself through these texts as a man of a broken heart with a paint brush and an endless supply of paint. He's raw and deep though simple with a light vocabulary. Even on the posted photos of half-naked women he will jot these poems. Though, they are not funny. They almost elude away from being sad. In an unsettling way, they're dark and scary. The simplicity he portrays is his master. No hindsight nor self-reflection will bother this brute. He's blunt and surface. He's black and mean and full of hate. Surprise me not would you tell me he writes through tears every time. He's possessed but not in a biblical sense, more through anger and fear and pure passion! He's dangerous, now more than I knew him before. He's a threat to himself and all those around him. He's a threat to Schoenfeld. Though, this is a good year ago now, who knows what could have become this situation. I'm left staring this monster in the eye. Saturated with evil are his intentions. Horrid wickedness beholds his doings. His lifeless gaze across my glass screen. A selfie in which he's made for us. "You're welcome" he decides. "Gaze upon me, I implore you" he insists. There's nothing safe in these feelings. My new understanding of his hurt, pained, and reckless state, plus his dangerous collection of iron, I fear for Schoenfeld greater than before.

I excuse myself from the meeting and head for my car in a quiet freak. I must retire home so that I can obsess over this matter further. My body aches along with my head. I can't seem to pass this. It must run its course. Home now, I retreat to my square of a room. Immediately on about my phone back into the den of chaos. Schoenfeld. Dear, sweet Schoenfeld. What has become you? Oh, my heart has folded and died for you in a form beyond any of my experience. To the picture of the smoking delinquent, I cast sympathy to a stranger of my memory, though, I feel I've gotten to know her in the past 24 hours. The real her. A disaster of a women rendered by threat and unfortunate catastrophe. I fear @papadiam had a leading role in Schoenfeld's final Instagram days. I fear he and she were a unit, a unit of chaos, and with her unknowing, he would wreak havoc unto her. She's scream to his roar, trip to his trap, prey to his predator.

This monster of a man demonstrates great control. Great manipulation. I know not of this fiend, though I abhor him deeply. His skin is tight and shiny. His teeth are sharp like knives. Of his body, crippling, crackling, hissing, mashing. A true, hideous, monstrous of being. He slings his prey and twines and rolls them. Suffocating and then sucking their blood. Injecting venom to infuse and create zombies whom only live for the little death. Insidiously lurks and recluses away into his pit amongst the bones of those lost in the fray. His legs are strong, skinny and quick. His arms are built and full of veins and atop his shoulders lay wicked of a spider thing. He waits in his funnel for vibration. Disgusting, hideous monster. I know it was you! I can't stand the thought, carnage of an angling widower, skulking about, creating insects helpless. I stand away from my device and sit to myself. A breath of deep air enters my body. It hits my lowest lungs then exhales. A beat persists in this moment. Calming of a breath it was, I turn to create a note of therapy. Finally, a moment of relief. All is now quiet outside and in. Sweat drips from my brow. Exhaustion takes me. Nonetheless, I place my hands among the stripes of black and white. The keys at my finger tips and all await the score of creation through the numbness of my mind. Schoenfeld, this one's for you.

Photo 3

"The Ass Shot"

I play in deep speculation of her final days about her account. Thoughts persist. Horrible thoughts, angry, hateful thoughts of her possible outcome. Though, as of now, I'm able to subdue the *fovos*. I continue about my day in this numb, tiresome state. I can quickly see how some if not most become addicted to types of melancholy. I sift unconsciously. "Going through the motions" as they say. I make my way to the window and stare blankly. No use of eyes when the mind controls all. And the mind does indeed control all. In my heart I search. All is clear now as my mind has rebooted. The fear of Schoenfeld's outcome being tragic is disheartening. But there is still a possibility that she's alive. Perhaps she's still only enslaved. Perhaps the spider of @papadiam has yet to commit his final deed of consumption. Or even perhaps he's completely lost interest and has left her. Left her to rot. Left her for dead! It's clear to me now. Whatever Schoenfeld's possible state, I must act as though she remains. I cannot give up on her now! Fate has a second chance.
Now in full effect, the crew and I begin to track down friends of Schoenfeld in hopes to come upon a lead of her possible whereabouts. We explain vaguely why we're doing it, that we're making a documentary about finding her. Hidden away are the true reasons of this escapade to not only these bystanders but my crew alike. It would be seen as crazy if I were single-handedly trying to hunt this woman down. And I'm not crazy, I'm just curious. I don't need to explain myself to you, you know, you've read everything up until now.

Continuing on. We meet with at least five different people, all around the same vicinity, and none of them claim to know Schoenfeld personally. Doubt begins to settle in. But I can't accept defeat just yet, I just don't know what else to try. After some time, I begin personally calling random individuals (all still from Instagram. After finding their information through searching) trying to explain my dilemma. Most of them hang up before I can even utter a phrase. A lot don't even answer the call. It's futile.

The day has been called and the crew retires home. I'm left thinking, but thankfully not anxiously. I sit to myself on my futon. I think about Schoenfeld. What kind of person would she be today? The once "Like him, he's ugly" trouble of a teenager could have a whole new ray to her. Did she fall further down the rabbit hole in anger and sadness. Did she learn nothing from her days of adolescence? Did she stray away from social norms with a disregard to empathy. Or did she become that of the opposite spectrum. Kind, nice, sweet, caring, loving. These thoughts hardly take heed, as I have nothing to base her off except her stupid Instagram account. Speaking of which, I haven't looked at it since yesterday. Might as well check, in case of any updates. I navigate to her page to find no news. But I stay on it for a while, almost mesmerized. I've seen all these photos and am familiar with them all but something strikes me as new. Not as physical but in essence. Is there actually something to these seemingly mindless posts? I pull up a picture of her taking a mirror selfie while she's pulling down the rear of her pants revealing her butt. Her face is slightly cut off (you see not her eyes). In the photo is a sink and on either side lay a cup and a mug. Near the mug is two used up bars of hand soap, one blue, on top of a white, both inside a same blue color dish. The lighting is a dim orange, only that of the bathroom light. Her blouse is a choice of floral fashion, red roses in bloom on a black back drop. She also wears a loose, wispy white cardigan sweater as it's slowly beginning to roll off her shoulders. Her brown hair is down and nothing special. The mirror she's in is of medium-small size, framed in a thrift shop gold/brown edging. Looking closer, I notice the nozzle of the sink is turned around facing away from the bowl. I'm unsure of the significance to this. And the caption says only "NSFW". This pursues back to my first theory of her.

The way the photo is framed in a raw and disregarded fashion. Along with the happenings inside the photo then tied off with the caption. I'm in doubt no longer. I deem this young woman as an artist. I continue skimming through her pieces. The next photo is that of a skyscraper in an upward Dutch-angle. It's a white building and a blue sky with an overall blue tone. It was probably taken with a cool white balance, though, it could also be a filter. The composition of the shot is dead-on and the caption is "tag your friends". Another is a shot of a little girl holding a large dead fish as she's attempting to feed it a drink. The caption is "hush rittle bb". They continue on like this. There are a lot of landscape photos and strange selfies. The captions are all so random which creates a pattern, rendering them as not random at all. At the start of her account, it was nothing but photography. Though, as her profile progressed, the subjects lean closer to smoking. Nicotine and marijuana alike. In late 2016 is when I notice her eyes die and at the same time, the spider of @papadiam creeps into her comments.

The peace of my silence is interrupted by the thoughts of the spider's influence on this poor girl. My mind plays out Schoenfeld awaiting her fate. She sits in a room, already stung by the spider's venom. She's limp. She slumps to the catch of the couch now at the mercy of what is to come. Out of the funnel, a master of puppets crawling on his strings. Only in a blur can she see a wretched outcome of a man. One certain step after the other, he grows through the hallway. His spider head glides in the air, licking the walls with its legs. Schoenfeld can't move. Her eyes show no distress though. She's unable to comprehend the moment. "This poison feels masterful in my blood". She's in dire danger. The spider crawls up next to her on the couch. With superior vision, he watches her. He watches right through her. It's a horror show. She's doomed. A feast is at hand. She's alone to her fate.

I snap myself out of this day-nightmare. Wretched of a place my mind is off to. I must call Dylan. With no time wasted, he answers, listens to my new idea, and decides to make his way over. With not a crew, he records the next set of sequences himself. I explain that I will instead of looking for Schoenfled, search for @papadiam, in hopes Schoenfeld will come. I find nothing on him specifically. He too disappeared in late 2016. I look up and search the people that consistently comment on his page. I call and call and call, with no prevail. Some answer, only to have no information. Hours go by as it becomes a dead trail. We nearly give up when my phone begins to ring. I glance to Dylan.

We're in disbelief. I peer down to the inevitable. An ominous hold captures through this device. Dylan rolls. I answer. "Hello?" "Are you the guy looking for Jose?" "I am" I respond. He then continues by disclosing information about where @papadiam lives, though this particular individual hasn't heard from him for as long as @papadiam's account has been inactive. I hang up the phone. We've got him! I search around the internet for a while in hopes to find a phone number to his residence. No luck. I then look up his abode on the maps app. It's not far from where I live. Only about 30 minutes into the mountains. A known to be sketchy area. Dylan and I set a date to visit the nest of the spider of @papadiam. Dylan then brings something to the front of his mind. Something that was better left unsaid. He feels as though I've become something of obsessed with this odyssey. He feels as though I'm only in it for some sort of self-want, as though the film is just a back drop to my true desires. He even goes as far as accusing me of falling in love with her. In love with Schoenfeld! "I don't even know her!" I exclaim! How could I possibly fall for someone I've never even met. Okay, I've met her once "Like him, he's ugly" but I never even uttered a single letter of a damn word back to her! In love? In love! Ha! What a damn joke! How now do I assure him that this project means nothing to me other than what the project means without him not believing me? An argument sparks as I try and defend what's left of my now damaged dignity. We all have our own ways of working. Why can't we just let it be as that? He then insists that he was wrong and tries to make amends but I looked deep into his eyes. He didn't even believe himself. For some odd reason, he's questioned my sanity. A reason in

which I haven't come to see. We confirm again on a date in which to reach @papadiam. Then he leaves.
Days pass and I just remain to myself. Anticipation takes place of my usual illness. If I could pace for days, I would but instead I opt out of much needed sleep as something of a tradition. I attempt to ready my body and my mind. Setting all equipment in ready and scarfing down meals of necessity. The day finally arrives. The day in which we hunt down the women-eating spider. I return to Schoenfeld's account one final time before I commit to this journey. And like my own fair maiden, she waits for me on the other side of the screen. Close enough to touch. Close enough to feel. I'm almost there, Katie.

Dylan shows up with only half the crew (not everybody is able to make it). Everything is locked and loaded. We set out on our way. The drive there is surreal and I think we all treat it with respect. Life somewhat stands still in this moment. I'm about to find out what has become of this women I've oddly been taken with. We enter the mountain as the trees scoop us up and then add cover over head. It becomes immediately dark as the shade has no regard for the light. As we drive deeper into the ominous back woods of our otherwise safe community, a fear sets in. It strikes true and is embedded in the very midst of our souls. From the looks of the others faces, I know I'm not the only one. The maps application directs us to now veer down a deep and narrow dirt road. This furthers us into blackness and something of a despair. "You have arrived" it warns us. Nobody is immediate to travel outside the car. I look around to grasp an understanding of our situation. To our right is the den of the spider of @papadiam. I step out of the car.

In the back hatchback, I begin setting up video and audio equipment. Chris, who's along with us, does the same. I multitask as I can't help myself from looking into the yard. It's eerily familiar. Without too much thought, I hand off the camera to a pair of hands receptive to take it. I return to Schoenfeld's account. I sift again through the sea of once random photos when I find one of her next to a car in a beat down yard. Caption: "me n bbis new cah". I look up. We're in the same place. Both satisfaction and dread sink into my lower stomach. "Is this the place?" asks Dylan. I reply "Yes". I begin to make my way around the fence but not inside. I'm to gather and collect a view of the land. Dylan and Chris stay behind at the car, still readying equipment. My eyes scan the yard. The ground is all dirt and small gravel rocks, decorated with larger boulders. There is a fire pit almost near the center of the yard itself. There's some type of chicken wire fencing collecting what is possibly chickens in a pen. Though, I can't see or hear any animal. The yard is pretty immense as it sinks down into the back where there's an old shed. I can't see inside as the windows are blacked out. To my left is the main house. It's old and ghastly, definitely not maintained. A large tree stands next to the run-down house, covering almost the entire property. To summarize it, it's a terrifying display of white trash. Dylan and Chris are ready.

They begin to roll as I enter the front gate. In this moment of pure slow motion, I remember the fear. It's thick and sour. It's harsh and abrupt. My palms begin to sweat and my breathing becomes shallow. In these tiny steps I call upon myself to talk me out of it. To all of whom this may mean, in all covers of sanity, I wish to be one of you, though, I know I'm far from telling the truth. I'm disrupted by my own terror, or the terror in which I let become me. Though, I feel as if the control of my own emotions have withered. I'm falling apart. In these tiny steps towards the monster's domain, I'm deconstructing. Knowing he will sense any slight momentum towards a faltering confidence. I question whether it is wise to move on. When it all leads up to this, am I what this creates me? Will this override the potency of my rescue for Schoenfeld? In these tiny steps, my character is challenged. Who am I? What am I, what am I made of? I'm not strong, or brave, or confident enough for this. But I can't just turn away. I need to stand. If not for myself, then, for somebody else. For Schoenfeld. If I could just fake it and pretend, just to get through it. But my fear is he will know I'm affected by this situation. Then I remember, I'm an actor, I can act like I'm unaffected.

So I put on my mask and begin taking larger steps all the way up to this fiend's door. With girth of a thud, I knock. Dylan and Chris remain rolling. They know not of what is to come from this. Same as me, though, taking on this role, the fear has hidden away. A beat passes. Nobody answers. I knock, again. Then suddenly, Dylan cuts to an update. He points to the mail box. It's full. As though no one has been here for a while. We look through, to date these notes. One of the last envelopes was in mid-2017. Did my trail just end. This can't be! Though Dylan and Chris advise against my doing, I rush, trudging into the house only to find nothing. No one is home, nor has anyone seemed to be living here for some time. Is this it? Is this all? Is there nothing to come from this? My eyes hold on a gaze-less stare when my mind begins to drift away. I've failed you, Schoenfeld. A month later, Dylan the crew and I are going over a new project idea. It's nothing really special as it's not holding my attention. I begin to stare off into space when a thought crosses my mind. There was nothing we did with that mockumentary. We just kind of scrapped it because it all amounted to nothing. My mind is in soup. I'm still frustrated about the happenings leading up to our anticlimactic end. Still disconnected to the committee, I decide to return to Schoenfeld's account. It's been at least a month since my last visit. I navigate to her profile to my great surprise. She's posted a new photo! The photo is a P.O.V. shot from her phone looking down toward a kitchen counter. Her free hand seems to be stuck in a Pringles jar. She's wearing leisure shorts and slip on uggs. There's a phone charger that's also on the counter and a loaf of bread in a bag. The caption is "halp me". I think to myself. I obviously realize this is stupid. It's just a moronic picture of her doing something bland while she's bored. It makes me think then, was that every single photo that she's ever taken on this stupid, waste of a time account? I try not to put too much thought into it as I just gaze back off to the open free air. A blissful moment plays by when my mind inevitably puts a halt to it. Ambiguity. I slowly begin tilting my head back down to the device. I cast sight upon the infernal waste of her profile. Back at the image of her hand in the Pringles jar. Again with the caption "halp me". Halp me? Fear reignites! What do you mean "halp me", Schoenfeld?

We're done

thank you for reading along and diving into my world.

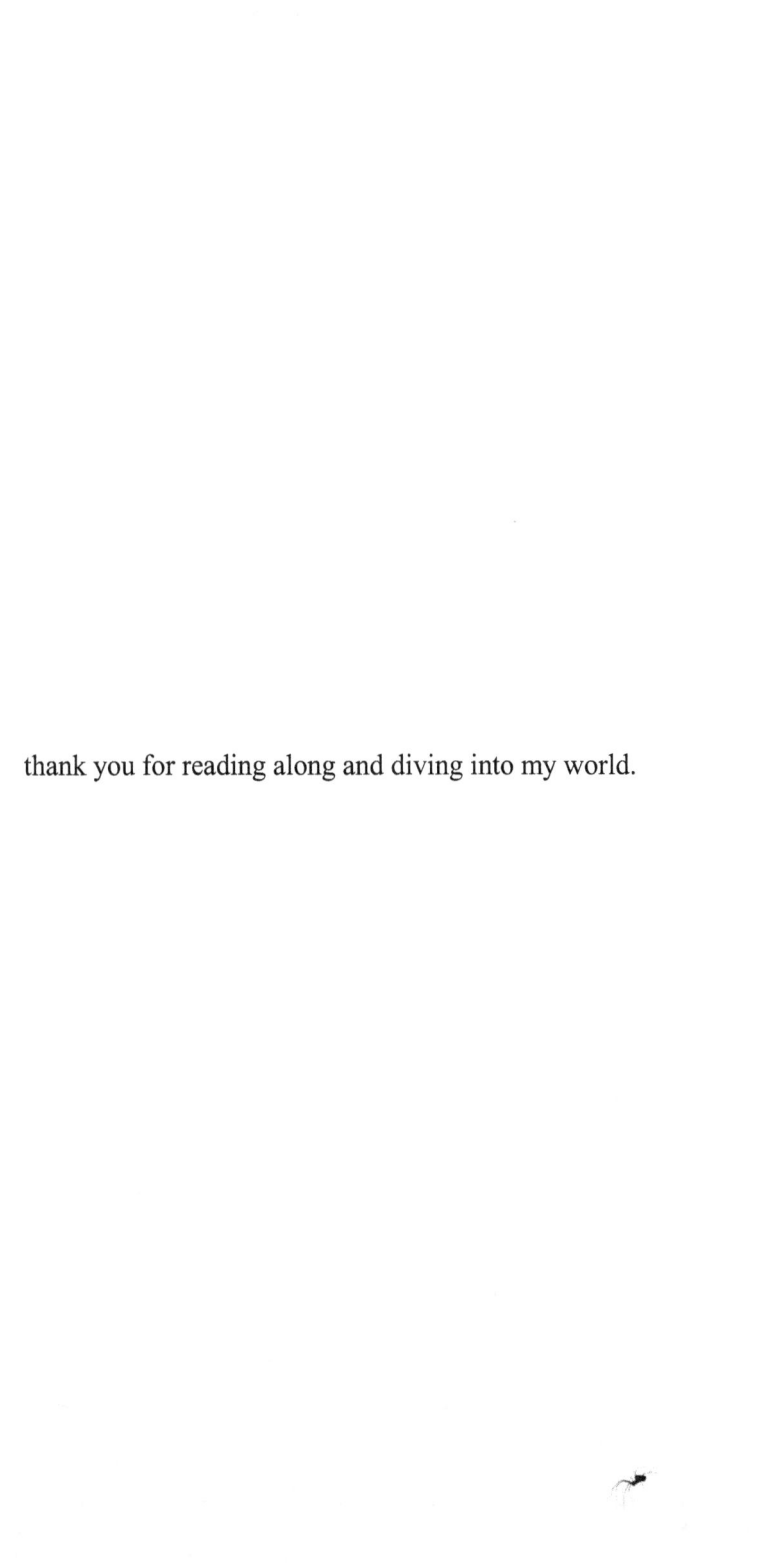